**GAO**

Report to Congressional Requesters

I0426413

May 2012

SEAFOOD SAFETY

Responsibility for Inspecting Catfish Should Not Be Assigned to USDA

GAO
Accountability ★ Integrity ★ Reliability

GAO-12-411

May 2012

GAO
Accountability * Integrity * Reliability

Highlights

Highlights of GAO-12-411, a report to congressional requesters

SEAFOOD SAFETY

Responsibility for Inspecting Catfish Should Not Be Assigned to USDA

Why GAO Did This Study

Since 2007, federal oversight of food safety has been on GAO's list of high-risk areas, largely because of fragmentation that has caused inconsistent oversight, ineffective coordination, and inefficient use of resources. The Food, Conservation, and Energy Act of 2008 (Farm Bill) further fragmented the food safety system by directing FSIS to issue catfish inspection regulations. FSIS prepared a risk assessment to determine risks associated with catfish and identified *Salmonella* as the primary food safety hazard in catfish. The Farm Bill split responsibility for seafood safety between FSIS, for catfish inspection, and FDA, for seafood generally; in addition, NMFS provides fee-for-service inspections of seafood-processing facilities. GAO was asked to examine FSIS's proposed catfish inspection program.

GAO examined (1) how FSIS determined that *Salmonella* presented the primary food safety hazard in catfish and (2) the anticipated impact of FSIS's proposed catfish inspection program on other federal food safety inspection programs. GAO reviewed FSIS's proposed catfish program and related documents and interviewed officials from FSIS, FDA, and other agencies.

What GAO Recommends

Congress should consider repealing provisions of the Farm Bill assigning USDA responsibility for catfish inspection. USDA stated it is committed to completing the rulemaking process on catfish inspection consistent with the 2008 Farm Bill provisions.

View GAO-12-411. For more information, contact Lisa Shames at (202) 512-3841 or shamesl@gao.gov.

What GAO Found

In determining that *Salmonella* is the primary food safety hazard in catfish, the U.S. Department of Agriculture's Food Safety and Inspection Service (FSIS) officials stated that the agency focused on *Salmonella* at the direction of the Office of Management and Budget (OMB), which considered *Salmonella* the most practical hazard to evaluate. However, GAO found that FSIS used outdated and limited information in its risk assessment as its scientific basis for a catfish inspection program that seeks to mitigate that hazard. For example, FSIS identified a single outbreak of *Salmonella*-caused illnesses, but this outbreak was not clearly linked to catfish. FSIS noted that this outbreak was before the Food and Drug Administration's (FDA) 1997 Seafood Hazard Analysis and Critical Control Point regulations, which required firms to identify hazards in their processing systems and implement controls to prevent or mitigate these hazards; no similar outbreaks have occurred since. Other federal agencies questioned if FSIS had adequately demonstrated a *Salmonella* problem in catfish. For example, FDA does not generally have such concerns. Officials with the National Oceanic and Atmospheric Administration's National Marine Fisheries Service (NMFS) also stated that FSIS did not adequately demonstrate that *Salmonella* was a problem with catfish.

With the implementation of FSIS's proposed catfish inspection program, responsibility for overseeing seafood safety would be further divided and would duplicate existing federal programs at a cost. Under FSIS's proposed program, processers would implement written sanitation and hazard control plans; FSIS would conduct continuous inspections of domestic catfish processing; and for imported catfish—which equal about 3 percent of all seafood imports—foreign countries would need to demonstrate equivalence to U.S. standards. According to FSIS, implementing this program will cost the government and industry about $14 million annually. If FSIS's proposed program were implemented, GAO expects it would cause duplication and inefficient use of resources in several key areas. First, the program requires implementation of hazard analysis plans that are essentially the same as FDA's hazard analysis requirements. Second, if the program is implemented, as many as three agencies—FDA, FSIS, and NMFS—could inspect facilities that process both catfish and other types of seafood. Both FDA and NMFS officials stated that continuous inspection will not improve catfish safety and is counter to the use of FDA's hazard analysis requirements, in which systems are most efficiently monitored periodically rather than daily. Third, the FDA Food Safety Modernization Act (FSMA) gives FDA authority to establish a system to accredit third party auditors, including foreign governments, to certify imported seafood meets FDA regulatory requirements. FDA officials stated that this new authority complements FDA's existing authority to obtain assurances about the safety of seafood exports from countries with food safety systems FDA determined are comparable to the United States. Under these systems more than catfish could be covered. With FDA's new authority under FSMA, the federal government has an opportunity to enhance the safety of all imported seafood—including catfish—and avoid the duplication of effort and cost that would result from FSIS's implementation of its proposed program.

Contents

Abbreviations

Farm Bill	Food, Conservation, and Energy Act of 2008
FDA	Food and Drug Administration
FSIS	Food Safety and Inspection Service
FSMA	FDA Food Safety Modernization Act
HACCP	Hazard Analysis and Critical Control Point
NMFS	National Marine Fisheries Service
OMB	Office of Management and Budget
USDA	U.S. Department of Agriculture

United States Government Accountability Office
Washington, DC 20548

May 10, 2012

The Honorable John D. Rockefeller, IV
Chairman
Committee on Commerce, Science, and Transportation
United States Senate

The Honorable Olympia J. Snowe
Ranking Member
Subcommittee on Oceans, Atmosphere, Fisheries, and Coast Guard
Committee on Commerce, Science, and Transportation
United States Senate

The Honorable Maria Cantwell
United States Senate

The Honorable Daniel K. Inouye
United States Senate

Since 2007, federal oversight of food safety has remained on our list of
high-risk areas in need of broad-based transformation to achieve greater
economy, efficiency, effectiveness, accountability, and sustainability,[1]
largely because of fragmentation that has caused inconsistent oversight,
ineffective coordination, and inefficient use of resources. The Department
of Health and Human Services' Food and Drug Administration (FDA) and
the U.S. Department of Agriculture's (USDA) Food Safety and Inspection
Service (FSIS) have primary oversight responsibilities for the safety of the
domestic and imported food supply. FSIS has historically been
responsible for meat, poultry, and processed egg products, and FDA is
responsible for all other food, including seafood. In addition, the National
Oceanic and Atmospheric Administration's National Marine Fisheries
Service (NMFS), through its fee-for-service inspection program, assesses
seafood processors' compliance with federal regulations.

FDA has traditionally had oversight over the safety of all seafood,
including catfish. The Food, Conservation, and Energy Act of 2008 (Farm

---

[1]See GAO, *High-Risk Series: An Update*, GAO-11-278 (Washington, D.C.: February
2011), and *High-Risk Series: An Update*, GAO-07-310 (Washington, D.C.: January 2007).

Bill), which was enacted in June 2008 and provides for the continuation of many agriculture programs through September 2012, assigned regulatory responsibility for the inspection of catfish to USDA once the agency issues final regulations for a mandatory catfish inspection program. Until those final regulations are issued, USDA has no responsibility for catfish safety. Specifically, among other things, the Farm Bill requires USDA, through FSIS, to provide continuous inspection of domestic catfish, including the processing of these fish. The Farm Bill also requires that FSIS issue final regulations for this inspection program after providing a period for public comments and public meetings before it implements the catfish inspection program. Congressional committees are in the process of considering proposals for a new Farm Bill.

In February 2011, FSIS published and sought comments on a proposed rule outlining possible regulations for a new catfish inspection program. Among other things, FSIS's proposed program would require processers to implement written sanitation and hazard control plans; FSIS inspectors to conduct continuous inspection of domestic catfish processing; and for imported catfish, foreign countries would need to demonstrate equivalence to U.S. standards. Specifically, FSIS would have an inspector at the processing facility to monitor all aspects of domestic catfish processing, and for imported catfish, review the food safety systems of countries seeking to export catfish to the United States to determine whether the foreign systems are equivalent to the U.S. food safety system for catfish. FSIS sought public comments on (1) whether it should primarily regulate a type of catfish most commonly raised in the United States or whether the agency should regulate all catfish, including fish commonly farmed in southeastern Asian countries, such as Vietnam, and (2) the timing of the program's implementation. FSIS prepared a draft health risk assessment (risk assessment) that cited *Salmonella* as the primary food safety hazard in catfish and prepared a preliminary regulatory impact analysis (impact analysis) to examine the costs and benefits of the proposed regulations. FSIS is reviewing the comments it received on the proposed regulations and the data from subsequent catfish sampling studies from 2008 through 2011 to develop a baseline of contamination in catfish; the agency has not settled on a date to issue the final regulations.

Once FSIS issues the final regulations required by the Farm Bill, FSIS, FDA, and NMFS will all have roles in the federal oversight of seafood products. We have reported many times that fragmentation in the nation's food safety system results in inconsistent oversight, ineffective coordination, and inefficient use of resources. For example, we reported in February 2012 that overlap and duplication of federal programs results in inefficient use of taxpayer funds.[2] We also reported that reducing or eliminating fragmentation, overlap, or duplication could help agencies provide more efficient and effective services. We also stated that several duplication issues may require legislative action.

In this context, this report responds to your request that we examine FSIS's proposed catfish inspection program. Our objectives were to determine (1) how FSIS determined that *Salmonella* presented the primary food safety hazard in catfish and (2) the anticipated impact of FSIS's proposed catfish inspection program on other federal food safety inspection programs.

To address these objectives, we reviewed FSIS's proposed catfish inspection program and related documents, including the risk assessment and impact analysis. In addition, we reviewed written public comments on the proposed regulations provided by industry and consumer groups. We interviewed officials from FSIS involved in the development of the proposed regulations and officials from FDA, NMFS, and other federal agencies, as well as representatives from industry and consumer advocacy groups. We conducted site visits of two domestic processing facilities that process catfish and other seafood. We reviewed components and costs of FSIS's proposed catfish inspection program, FDA's seafood inspection program, and NMFS's fee-for-service seafood inspection program. Appendix I provides additional information on our scope and methodology.

We conducted this performance audit from June 2011 to May 2012 in accordance with generally accepted government auditing standards. Those standards require that we plan and perform the audit to obtain sufficient, appropriate evidence to provide a reasonable basis for our findings and conclusions based on our audit objectives. We believe that the evidence obtained provides a reasonable basis for our findings and conclusions based on our audit objectives.

---

[2]GAO, *2012 Annual Report: Opportunities to Reduce Duplication, Overlap and Fragmentation, Achieve Savings, and Enhance Revenue,* GAO-12-342SP (Washington, D.C.: Feb. 28, 2012).

Background

FSIS and FDA are the two primary food safety agencies. FSIS is responsible for the safety of meat, poultry, and processed egg products, and, pursuant to the Farm Bill, is given authority to inspect catfish as soon as it issues final regulations to carry out a catfish inspection program. FDA is responsible for virtually all other food, including seafood. Under the Federal Food, Drug, and Cosmetic Act, FDA is responsible for ensuring that the nation's food supply, including seafood, is safe, wholesome, sanitary, and properly labeled. Since 1997, FDA has used the internationally recognized Hazard Analysis and Critical Control Point (HACCP) system as its main oversight tool for seafood safety. FDA requires seafood processing firms—those that, among other things, manufacture, pack, or label seafood products—to use a HACCP system. Under this system, processors are primarily responsible for the safety of the seafood they process. That is, processors are responsible for identifying where in their processing system one or more hazards are reasonably likely to occur (hazard analysis) and implementing control techniques to prevent or mitigate these hazards. Processors are to lay out their hazard analysis and control techniques in HACCP plans. FDA verifies through inspections that the techniques are adequate to control the identified significant hazards and are being effectively implemented. FDA inspects domestic and foreign seafood processors in an effort to ensure their compliance with HACCP regulations. FDA supplements its HACCP oversight activities with an import oversight program that includes examination and testing of some imported seafood at ports of entry to ensure the products meet U.S. requirements, including the absence of residues of drugs that are unapproved for use in the United States and would render the seafood adulterated under the Federal Food, Drug, and Cosmetic Act; FDA also maintains data on the shipments of seafood that it has refused to allow into the United States.

The FDA Food Safety Modernization Act (FSMA), enacted in January 2011, gives FDA new authorities to improve its ability to oversee the safety of imported foods. As described in FSMA, FDA must establish a system for recognizing accreditation bodies to accredit third-party auditors, including foreign governments, to conduct food safety audits to determine compliance with the Federal Food, Drug, and Cosmetic Act and to certify that eligible foreign entities, including seafood processors, meet applicable requirements. FDA may directly accredit third-party auditors under certain circumstances.[3] FSMA also contains provisions on laboratory accreditation that enable FDA to leverage state, foreign government, and private laboratory resources for food testing. Furthermore, these laboratories must meet model standards developed by FDA that ensure quality and reliability of the test results used to verify the safety of any food product, including imports. In April 2011, we stated that FDA's current program to ensure the safety of imported seafood is limited because the agency relies on document review at individual foreign processing facilities and on importers for HACCP compliance, conducts only a few inspections of foreign facilities, samples a limited number of imports at the U.S. border, and does not make effective use of laboratory resources.[4] For example, in fiscal year 2011, FDA examined about 3.4 percent of all seafood entries and performed laboratory analysis on 0.7 percent of these entries. We recommended, in part, that FDA study the feasibility of adopting practices that the European Union employs to ensure the safety of imported seafood products, such as requiring foreign countries that want to export seafood to the United States to develop a national residues monitoring plan to control the use of drugs used in aquaculture (fish farming). Because fish grown in confined aquacultured areas can have high rates of bacterial infections, farmers may treat them with drugs, such as antibiotics and antifungal agents, to increase fish survival rates. According to a 2008 FDA report, the residues of some of these drugs can cause cancer, allergic reactions, and antibiotic resistance when consumed by humans. As imports of aquacultured seafood products increase, so do the concerns over the presence of drug residues.

NMFS's Seafood Inspection Program provides fee-for-service inspections, primarily under the authority of the Federal Agricultural Marketing Act of 1946. According to NMFS officials, NMFS's experience with seafood controls dates to the1970s, when the agency began systematically evaluating controls as part of its inspection program. NMFS more formally adopted the systematic evaluation with the development of its Quality Management Program in 1993, which

---

[3]If FDA has not identified and recognized an accreditation body to meet the requirements within 2 years of the establishment of the accreditation system, FDA can directly accredit third-party auditors.

[4]GAO, *Seafood Safety: FDA Needs to Improve Oversight of Imported Seafood and Better Leverage Limited Resources*, GAO-11-286 (Washington, D.C.: Apr. 14, 2011).

integrates quality into its HACCP-based inspection system. Currently, NMFS provides inspection services on request to the seafood industry—including domestic and foreign processors, distributors, and other firms—to certify that these seafood firms comply with HACCP requirements and other federal food safety standards, among other things. Some retailers require this certification as a condition for purchasing the seafood products.

Before 2002, various fish in the order *Siluriformes* were commonly labeled and sold as "catfish." However, in 2002, Congress amended the Federal Food, Drug, and Cosmetic Act to allow only fish from the family *Ictaluridae* (in the order *Siluriformes*) to use the name catfish in labeling. All other fish, such as those from the *Pangasiidae* family (in the order *Siluriformes*) that had previously been labeled as catfish, had to have other names on labels, such as basa, swai, or tra. In making catfish subject to mandatory FSIS inspection, the Farm Bill gave the Secretary of Agriculture discretion to define "catfish" for the purposes of inspection—that is, to distinguish between different types of catfish or to consider all fish in the order *Siluriformes* as catfish. For purposes of this report, we refer to all catfish potentially subject to regulations as catfish, including fish in the family *Ictaluridae*, which are primarily of domestic origin, and *Pangasiidae*, which come primarily from Vietnam (see fig. 1).

Figure 1: Typical Domestic and Imported Catfish

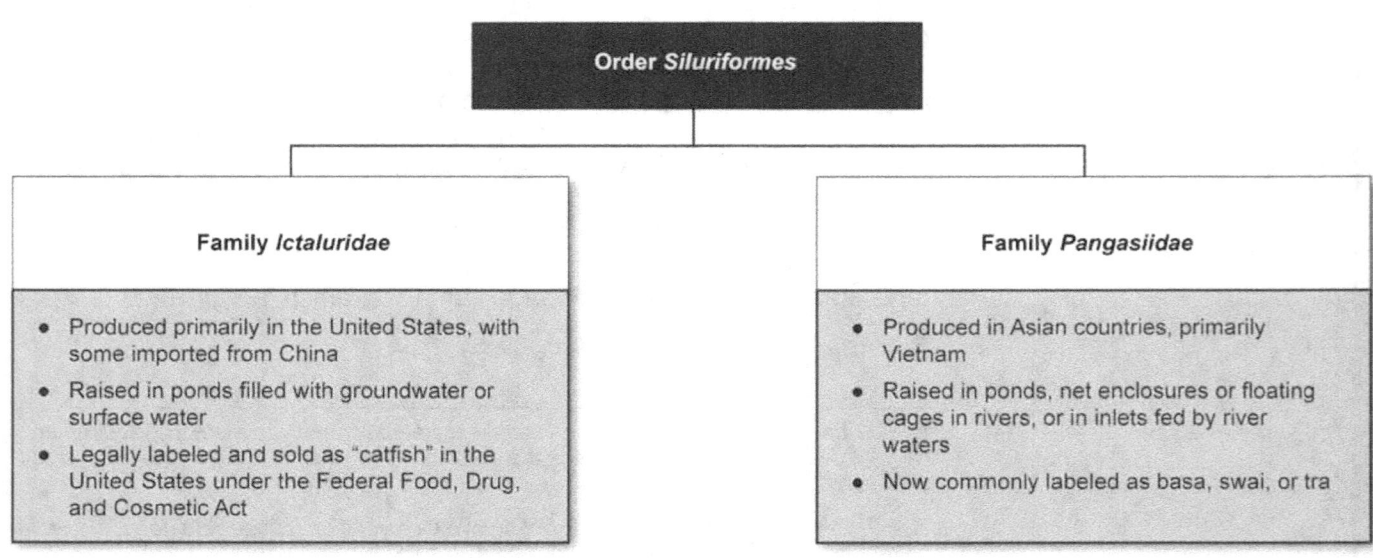

Source: GAO analysis.

In recent years, the volume of imported catfish of all families entering the U.S. market has continued to increase, while the volume of domestic catfish entering the market has declined. In 2002, the percentage of imported catfish in the U.S. market was estimated at 2 percent, and by 2006, imported catfish of all families accounted for an estimated 12 percent of the U.S. market. This trend has continued: by 2010, imported catfish accounted for 23 percent of the U.S. catfish market, and domestic catfish accounted for 77 percent. The most recent data show a 29-percent decline in domestic catfish production from 2010 to 2011. Figure 2 shows the trend in the volume of domestic and imported catfish from 2006 to 2010. Overall, imported Siluriformes catfish constituted a small fraction of seafood imported to the U.S. in 2010, at about 3 percent. Figure 3 shows the major countries exporting catfish to the United States.

Figure 2: Domestic and Imported Siluriformes Catfish in the U.S. Market

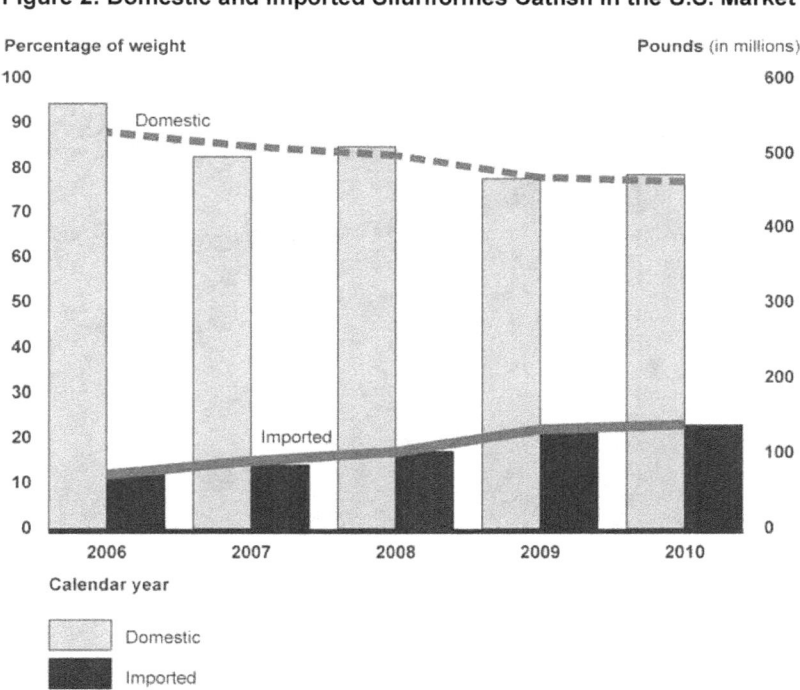

Sources: GAO analysis of USDA National Agricultural Statistics Service and U.S. Census Bureau data

Figure 3: Sources of Imported Siluriformes Catfish, 2010

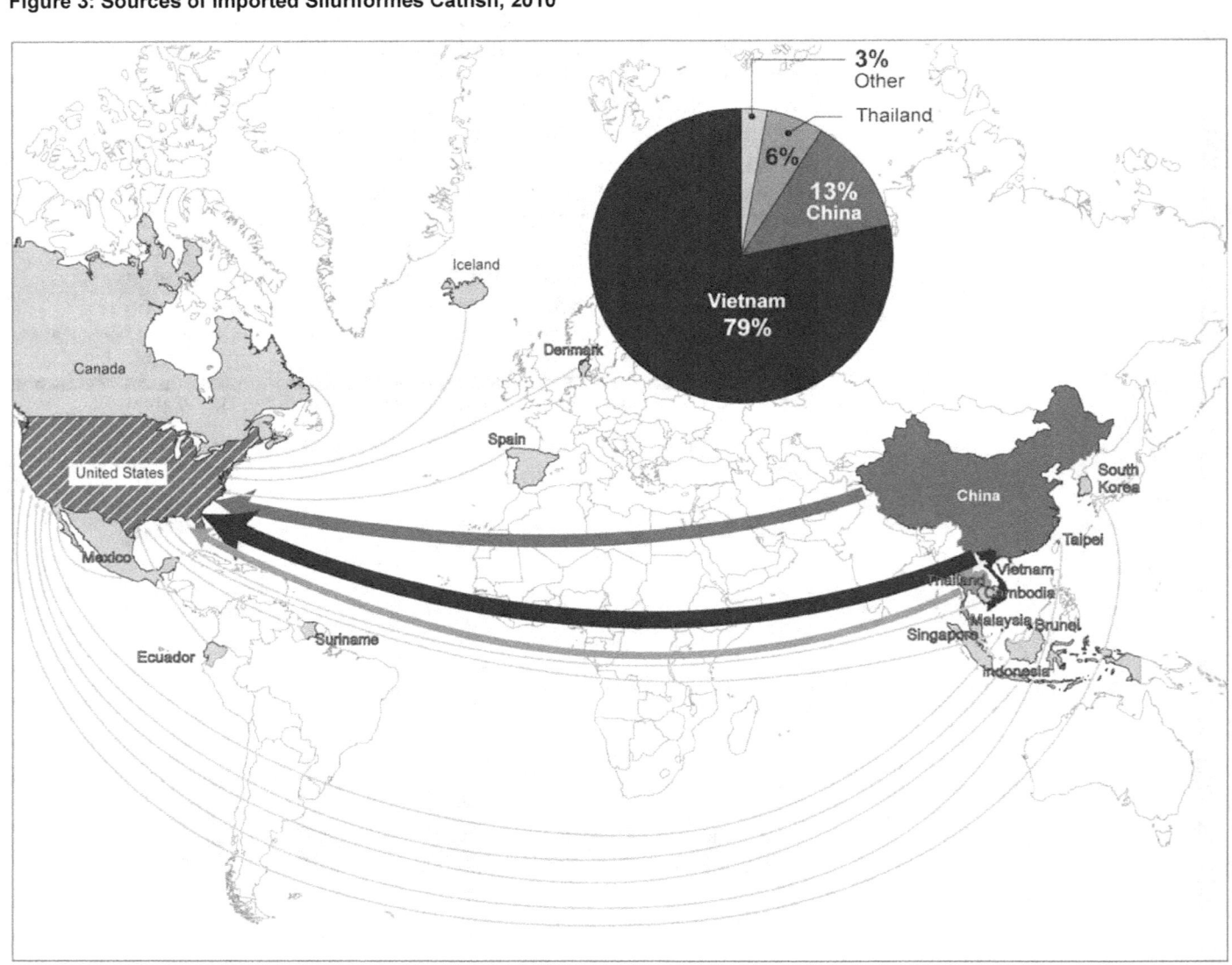

Sources: GAO analysis of Department of Commerce data and Map Resources (map)

Note: Percentages do not add to 100 percent due to rounding.

The volume of catfish subject to FSIS's proposed catfish inspection program will depend on the definition of catfish that the Secretary of Agriculture decides to apply. In 2010, 79 percent of the catfish in the U.S. market consisted primarily of domestically processed catfish as well as some imported catfish from the family *Ictaluridae*, while the remaining 21 percent consisted of imported catfish from the family *Pangasiidae*. If the Secretary of Agriculture chose to limit the definition to catfish to the family *Ictaluridae*, FSIS's inspection program would thus cover almost 80 percent of the catfish in the U.S. market in 2010.

The Farm Bill requires that FSIS issue the final regulations for its new catfish inspection program before it can begin inspecting catfish. Citing requirements of the Federal Crop Insurance Reform Act of 1994, FSIS prepared a risk assessment and an impact analysis and made them available for public review. FSIS used the risk assessment to determine the primary hazard of concern associated with consuming farm-raised catfish in the United States, and it conducted an impact analysis to examine the costs and benefits of the proposed regulations.[5] FSIS prepared these documents to evaluate the potential public health benefits of its proposed program if the primary hazard were addressed. The Federal Crop Insurance Reform and Department of Agriculture Reorganization Act of 1994 requires an analysis of the health risks and costs and benefits for major proposed regulations that regulate human health, human safety, or the environment (i.e., defined as regulations the Secretary of Agriculture estimates are likely to have an annual impact on the U.S. economy of $100 million in 1994 dollars). In addition, Executive Order 12866 established the guidance that agencies are to follow when developing regulations.[6] Under this guidance, agencies are to identify the problem new regulations are intended to address and evaluate the significance of the problem. The executive order further directs that the agencies consider the alternative of not regulating, but it recognizes that agencies should issue regulations as required by law, as are the regulations for the catfish inspection program. The executive order directs agencies to provide a description of the need for any significant regulatory action, how that action meets the needs, and the costs and benefits of the action. A significant regulatory action includes any regulatory action that has an annual effect on the economy of $100 million or more or adversely affects, among other things, the economy or a sector of the economy. Under the executive order, the Office of Management and Budget (OMB)

[5]Although FSIS characterized its risk assessment as "illustrative," the agency nonetheless focused on *Salmonella* as the most significant hazard associated with catfish.

[6]"Regulatory Planning and Review," Exec. Order No. 12866. 58 Fed. Reg. 51, 735 (Sept. 30, 1993).

has a review function to, among other things; ensure that regulations are consistent with principles set forth in the executive order.

FSIS Used Outdated Data to Justify its Determination

In determining that *Salmonella* is the primary food safety hazard in catfish, FSIS officials told us that the agency focused on *Salmonella* at the direction of OMB, which considered *Salmonella* the most practical hazard to evaluate. However, we found that FSIS used outdated and limited information as its scientific basis for implementing a catfish inspection program that was required by law.

According to FSIS, the agency initially focused its risk assessment of potential contaminants in catfish primarily on public health outcomes associated with chemical contaminants, with limited attention to *Salmonella*. (The appendix to FSIS's risk assessment includes information on these hazards.) However, upon reviewing the initial FSIS assessment, agency officials said that OMB directed FSIS to focus its catfish risk assessment on *Salmonella*, not as the "riskiest hazard" but as the "most practical" and to note that there was uncertainty regarding the sufficiency of information used to demonstrate the association between *Salmonella* and catfish. Furthermore, FSIS officials agreed that *Salmonella* was a practical choice, in part, because the agency could show that it is a major cause of illnesses in the United States, although not necessarily from catfish. For example, a 2011 report from the Department of Health and Human Services' Centers for Disease Control and Prevention stated that *Salmonella* infection causes more hospitalizations and deaths than any other bacteria and showed that the major sources of illnesses caused by *Salmonella* from 2004 to 2008 were poultry; eggs; pork; beef; and vine vegetables, fruits, and nuts. Moreover, the risk assessment cited FSIS's knowledge and experience working with *Salmonella* detection and prevention, but that its knowledge and experience related to poultry, not seafood.

According to FSIS officials, because of OMB direction and availability of information, FSIS identified *Salmonella* as the primary hazard for catfish in its risk assessment. FSIS's risk assessment stated it assumed that the prevalence of the identified primary hazard associated with catfish was the same for domestic and foreign catfish. The risk assessment cited the following to support the claim that *Salmonella* in catfish was the primary hazard:

- *Salmonella* may be a concern with catfish because catfish are raised in fish farms, and *Salmonella* is a potential microbial hazard for aquatic environments.

- *Salmonella* is a high-priority hazard and of great concern in the United States because of the general burden of illnesses associated with it. In particular, FSIS's risk assessment stated that the Centers for Disease Control and Prevention had identified a 1991 *Salmonella* outbreak in which catfish may have been the source.

- A 1979 article in the *Journal of Food Science* indicated that *Salmonella* was found in 21 percent of catfish collected from ponds and retail markets.[7]

- A 1998 research study found that 2 percent of catfish fillets collected from three processing facilities were contaminated with *Salmonella*. Researchers collected these catfish fillet samples between August 1994 and May 1995.[8]

- According to an analysis by USDA's Economic Research Service of FDA data on imports that were denied entry into the United States from 1998 to 2004 (i.e., import refusal data), about 42 percent of the violations listed for imported catfish were for *Salmonella*.[9]

The following describes limitations we identified in FSIS's rationale for designating *Salmonella* as the basis for regulation:

- A 2010 United Nations Food and Agriculture Organization report on *Salmonella* contamination in aquaculture stated that products from fish farms are rarely involved in outbreaks of illnesses caused by

---

[7]Wyatt, L.E., Nickelson, R. II, & Vanderzant, C., "Occurrence and Control of *Salmonella* in Freshwater Catfish," *Journal of Food Science*, vol. 44 (1979), 1067-1073.

[8]McCaskey, T., Hannah, T.C., Lovell, T., Silva, J.L., Fernandes, C.F., & Flick, G.J., "Safe and Delicious Study Shows Catfish is Low Risk for Foodborne Illness," *Highlights of Agricultural Research*, vol. 45, no. 4 (1998).

[9]U.S. Department of Agriculture, Economic Research Service, *Economic Research Service Staff Analysis of FDA Import Refusals for Catfish, 1998-2004* (Washington, D.C., 2009).

Salmonella. In addition, even when a low prevalence of *Salmonella* is present, thorough cooking will eliminate the hazard.[10]

- FSIS's risk assessment provided one example of a *Salmonella* outbreak associated with catfish consumption. This outbreak occurred in 1991, and the Centers for Disease Control and Prevention was not completely sure that catfish was the source of the *Salmonella* that resulted in the illnesses. For example, coleslaw was also consumed along with catfish and could have been the source of the *Salmonella*.

- The 1998 study cited in FSIS's risk assessment concluded that the health hazards from *Salmonella* and other bacteria in catfish were practically zero because the incidence in catfish was low and because catfish are cooked prior to consumption.

- Most of the information listed earlier and used by FSIS to support *Salmonella* as the primary hazard associated with catfish was compiled before 1997, when FDA required seafood processing facilities to implement HACCP systems. According to FDA documents, HACCP regulations initiated a landmark program to reduce seafood-related illnesses to the lowest possible levels. In its proposed catfish inspection regulations, FSIS acknowledged the impact of HACCP controls, stating that the one outbreak it identified occurred before FDA's implementation of HACCP regulations. It also noted that since HACCP implementation, no cases of illnesses caused by *Salmonella* and linked to catfish have been reported.

- In a subsequent report, USDA's Economic Research Service stated the analysis of FDA import refusal data that it provided to FSIS indicating a catfish violation rate of about 42 percent has its limitations and does not reflect the true violation level because this information is not based on a random sampling of imports. Rather, it reflects FDA's focus on areas with past compliance problems, such as companies and products.[11] In addition, in commenting on FDA's import samples, FSIS stated in its risk assessment that the limitations of the catfish

---

[10]United Nations, Food and Agriculture Organization, *FAO Expert Workshop on the Application of Biosecurity Measures to Control Salmonella Contamination in Sustainable Aquaculture*, Fisheries and Aquaculture Report No. 937 (Mangalore, India, January 2010).

[11]U.S. Department of Agriculture, Economic Research Service, *Economic Research Service Staff Analysis of FDA Import Shipments, Refusals, and Violations for Catfish and Non-Ictalurus Fish. January 1, 1998-August 21, 2010* (Washington, D.C., 2011).

data would likely overestimate the prevalence of *Salmonella* contamination in catfish. FSIS also stated in its risk assessment that FDA sampling and testing limitations made reasonable assumptions about the prevalence of *Salmonella* in imported catfish nearly impossible.

- Preliminary results of microbiological testing FSIS conducted in 2011 to establish a baseline for *Salmonella* in catfish indicated the presence of *Salmonella* in over 1 percent of the total catfish samples taken in the study. This is lower than the presence of *Salmonella* identified in studies and other data sources that FSIS cited in its risk assessment (e.g., FDA import refusal data).

FSIS stated in its risk assessment that data were limited regarding the prevalence of catfish contaminated with *Salmonella*. Furthermore, it stated there was substantial uncertainty about the number of illnesses caused by *Salmonella* that could be attributed to catfish consumption. Moreover, a peer-reviewed journal article by agency staff stated that scientific literature on foodborne hazards associated with catfish was limited and dated. The article added that extensive studies were needed to establish the baseline prevalence of *Salmonella* in catfish.[12]

FDA and NMFS, which each have about 14 years experience in inspecting catfish processing facilities under HACCP regulations, as well as experience in sampling catfish products, also questioned whether FSIS had adequately demonstrated that *Salmonella* in catfish was a problem. According to FDA and NMFS officials, FSIS did not provide any new information or data in its risk assessment indicating that catfish was unsafe to consume or that the current oversight system was not addressing any potential problems. According to FDA officials, based on the agency's experience and information from its own testing programs, catfish is a low-risk product, and the agency generally does not have any concerns related to *Salmonella* in catfish. According to NMFS officials, FSIS did not adequately demonstrate that *Salmonella* was a significant problem with catfish because data are not available to confirm this

---

[12]Erica McCoy, Jaime Morrison, Victor Cook, John Johnston, Denise Eblen, and Chuanfa Guo, "Foodborne Agents Associated with the Consumption of Aquaculture Catfish," *Journal of Food Protection*, vol. 74, no. 3, (2011), pages 500-516. Risk Assessment Division, Office of Public Health Science, U.S. Department of Agriculture, Food Safety and Inspection Service. Washington, D.C.

hazard. NMFS added that it was more likely that unapproved veterinary drugs and chemical residues were the hazards most associated with catfish. According to its proposed regulations, FSIS considered several other hazards it thought might be associated with catfish.[13]

FSIS's Proposed Program Mirrors Existing Programs, Introducing Overlap and Inefficiencies

FSIS's proposed catfish inspection program would further divide responsibility for overseeing seafood safety and introduce overlap at considerable cost. In our March 2011 report, we cited FSIS's catfish inspection program as an example of further fragmentation of the food safety system.[14] In reviewing the proposed catfish program, we identified four areas that raise concerns about the potential for overlap or inefficient use of resources if FSIS were to implement the catfish inspection program: (1) similar HACCP requirements, (2) inspection overlap and unnecessary frequency of inspection, (3) inconsistent oversight of imported seafood, and (4) the cost of implementing FSIS's catfish inspection program.

Similar HACCP requirements. FDA and NMFS require, and FSIS would require, facilities to implement HACCP systems to reduce the risk of illness from contaminated foods. Table 1 shows the requirements of a HACCP system for catfish and how each agency implements or would implement these requirements.

---

[13]The other hazards FSIS considered included heavy metals, pesticides, unapproved antimicrobials, *Listeria monocytogenes*, and Enterotoxigenic *E. coli*.

[14]GAO, *Opportunities to Reduce Potential Duplication in Government Programs, Save Tax Dollars, and Enhance Revenue*, GAO-11-318SP (Washington, D.C.: Mar. 1, 2011).

Table 1: FDA and NMFS HACCP Plan Requirements, and FSIS Proposed Requirements

	Division of Seafood Safety, FDA	Seafood Inspection Program, NMFS	Office of Catfish Inspection Program (proposed), FSIS
Statutory authority	Federal Food, Drug, and Cosmetic Act; Public Health Service Act	Agriculture Marketing Act of 1946	Federal Meat Inspection Act, as applicable to catfish
Written HACCP plan required	x	x	x
HACCP plan requirements			
List/identify chemical, physical, and biological safety hazards	x	x	x
List/identify critical control points (CCP)	x	x	x
List/identify critical limits for each CCP	x	x	x
List procedures to monitor each CCP including monitoring frequency	x	x	x
Include any corrective action plans	x[a]	x[a]	x[b]
Provide a recordkeeping system that documents the monitoring of CCPs	x	x	X
List verification procedures and frequency	x	x	x
Validate CCPs are effective in controlling hazards	X	x	x
Require written Sanitation Standard Operating Procedures	No written procedures required but processors must implement and monitor sanitation controls and maintain records	x	x
Preoperational sanitation evaluation conducted as part of inspection	Conducted as needed	x	x
Frequency of domestic site inspections	Every 3 to 5 years for products FDA considers low risk, such as catfish	Minimum, quarterly audits	On-site inspection during processing

Source: GAO analysis of FDA, NMFS, and FSIS program documents.

[a]Plans must include corrective action plans developed in accordance with the requirements of 21 C.F.R.§ 123.7.

[b]Plans must include corrective action plans developed in accordance with the requirements of 9 C.F.R. § 417.3.

As table 1 shows, the three agencies essentially do not differ from each other in their HACCP requirements. FSIS acknowledges that many domestic processing facilities are already meeting many of its proposed requirements. Nevertheless, if FSIS implements its proposed catfish program, catfish processors are likely to see their paperwork requirements increase. For example, FSIS would require written sanitation plans, while FDA inspectors do not require written sanitation plans and instead require only that sanitation be monitored and records kept, according to FDA officials. Therefore, catfish processing facilities without written sanitation plans would now be required to develop them. Catfish processing facilities that already contract for inspection services with NMFS must have written sanitation plans, but FSIS officials said the format of the FSIS sanitation plan would differ from the one already required by NMFS. FSIS officials noted that some of the additional paperwork burden required for FSIS regulations would be offset by the reduction of FDA paperwork requirements. However, facilities that process catfish and other seafood would be required to meet both FSIS and FDA paperwork requirements, which may differ. For instance, FSIS plans to develop its own forms for documenting a HACCP system, which will require processors of catfish and other seafood under FSIS and FDA oversight to enter the same information twice—once for FSIS and once for FDA.

Inspection overlap and unnecessary inspection frequency. FSIS's proposed catfish program would introduce inefficiencies into the U.S. catfish inspection system by duplicating existing FDA and NMFS inspections. Currently, about 18 major domestic facilities process catfish, according to FSIS, and an unknown number of facilities process both catfish and other seafood. With the implementation of FSIS's catfish inspection program, facilities that process only catfish may be inspected by FSIS and NMFS, and facilities that process both catfish and other seafood may be inspected by all three agencies—FSIS, FDA, and NMFS. FDA inspects facilities that process only catfish every 3 to 5 years because it considers catfish a low-risk product, but it may inspect other facilities that process catfish, along with other seafood, more frequently, depending on the risks associated with the other seafood. NMFS conducts a minimum of quarterly inspections of processing facilities that participate in its Quality Management Program, including a majority of the domestic catfish-processing facilities FSIS identified.[15] According to NMFS documents we reviewed, many retail and distribution firms buying processed catfish products currently require NMFS product verifications

---

[15]NMFS's Quality Management Program integrates HACCP preventive control strategies to ensure seafood is safe, complies with all food regulations, and meets internationally recognized quality standards.

and are likely to still require NMFS verification after promulgation of the FSIS proposed regulations. For example, representatives we spoke with from two domestic facilities that process catfish and other seafood told us that they expect to continue to pay for NMFS inspections to meet retailer demands, despite any additional oversight FSIS provides. In addition to any NMFS services that they retain, facilities that process both catfish and other seafood will also be required to meet both FDA and FSIS requirements and will be subject to inspections by both agencies. According to FSIS officials, overlap of programs is outside the agency's control because the proposed program was mandated by Congress.

Implementation of the proposed catfish inspection program would also fragment the export certification processes that some foreign governments require for the export of U.S.-produced seafood. Under its proposed regulations, FSIS would issue official export certificates for shipments of inspected and passed catfish products produced in the United States for export to foreign countries, as authorized by the Federal Meat Inspection Act. However, NMFS currently provides these certification services for all seafood, including catfish. According to NMFS officials, this dual certification creates a potential problem because NMFS already has approval from multiple foreign governments to serve as the U.S. certification authority for seafood exports.

FSIS's proposed use of continuous monitoring in the form of daily inspections for catfish is also unlikely to reduce the hazard of contamination in catfish as intended and is not risk based, according to FDA and NMFS officials. (Under the Farm Bill, FSIS is required to issue final regulations to conduct continuous monitoring of catfish processing facilities, as it does for meat, poultry, and processed egg products facilities). FDA officials told us FSIS's continuous monitoring approach is counter to HACCP-based requirements for seafood and not based on risk. According to FDA and NMFS officials, only periodic inspection is necessary to verify that a HACCP plan is being implemented and adequate preventive controls are in place. According to NMFS documents we reviewed, the current HACCP approach to seafood safety is fundamental not only in the United States but also in most seafood-producing countries around the world. Consequently, these countries rely on periodic, not daily, inspections. In addition, NMFS stated that continuous inspection will not enhance the level of safety with catfish because disease cannot be identified by visual inspection, as it can for meat and poultry. NMFS noted that because continuous or daily inspection does not necessarily improve seafood safety, its use is more costly with little effect.

We have reported on duplication and overlap in federal inspection of seafood in the past, when only FDA and NMFS were concerned. In 2009, we reported that FDA does not try to determine whether NMFS has already inspected a seafood facility when it is deciding which facilities to inspect.[16] In 2011, we reported that NMFS and FDA were still not coordinating their inspection activities.[17] Lack of coordination can burden seafood processors. For example, according to representatives of a facility that processes seafood, the facility was inspected approximately 21 times by NMFS, FDA, and USDA over a 4-year period, from 2005 to 2008, with no significant problems identified in any of the inspections.[18]

Inconsistent oversight of imported seafood. Consistent with the Federal Meat Inspection Act, as amended by the Farm Bill, FSIS plans to apply an equivalency approach for catfish that is similar to the one it uses for imported meat, poultry, and processed egg products. Under FSIS's equivalency approach, meat, poultry and processed egg products are not eligible for export to the United States unless FSIS has determined that the exporting country has a food safety system equivalent to that of the United States. Among other things, FSIS reviews documents provided by foreign governments, conducts on-site evaluations of government inspections of processing facilities, and audits laboratories to ensure their food safety regulations and oversight are adequate. In addition, FSIS reinspects products at U.S. ports of entry to promote compliance.

Some individuals and organizations that supported the transfer of catfish safety from FDA to FSIS, which include representatives of the catfish industry and consumer groups, stated that there were several problems with FDA's oversight system, such as limited inspection and sampling of imported seafood, and that FSIS's proposed catfish program regulations, if implemented, would enhance catfish safety. For example, in their written comments to FSIS, some supporters stated that imported catfish may be unsafe because they were raised under less stringent standards, such as allowing the catfish to be exposed to whatever pollutants were

---

[16]GAO, *Seafood Fraud: FDA Program Changes and Better Collaboration among Key Federal Agencies Could Improve Detection and Prevention*, GAO-09-258 (Washington, D.C., Feb. 19, 2009).

[17]GAO-11-286.

[18]USDA contracted with a private company to inspect this facility because the processing facility provided seafood products to federal child nutrition programs.

present in the river water where they were raised. Supporters also indicated that imported catfish may contain residues from drugs that FDA has not approved for use in aquaculture. Finally, supporters noted that FSIS staff would review foreign catfish safety systems to ensure these systems met U.S. requirements before such products were admitted into U.S. commerce. In addition, FSIS inspectors would reinspect catfish imports at the ports of entry.

In April 2011, we reported that FDA's oversight of imports is limited when compared with FSIS's more comprehensive reviews of food safety systems under its equivalence program.[19] However, FSMA gives FDA authority to establish a system to accredit third-party auditors, including foreign governments, to take responsibility for certifying seafood processors or seafood meets FDA regulatory requirements. Under this system, a foreign government would have to demonstrate that its food safety programs, systems, and standards are capable of adequately ensuring that the foreign government and the foods it certifies, including seafood, meet FDA requirements. According to FDA officials, its new FSMA authorities complement the authority it already had to conduct comparability assessments, which are intended to help ensure the safety of imported foods. With comparability assessments, FDA can leverage the work of foreign governments whose food safety systems FDA has determined provide protections that are comparable to those of the U.S. food safety system. FDA is currently piloting a comparability assessment process with the European Union and New Zealand. New authorities provided in FSMA, including third party certification, will enable FDA to leverage resources of countries with sufficient qualifications—even though they may not have comparable systems—to help ensure that foods exported to the United States meet FDA requirements. Enacted in 2011, these new FSMA authorities were not available to FDA when the Farm Bill assigned responsibility for catfish inspection to FSIS in 2008.

Cost of implementing FSIS's catfish inspection program. Currently, FDA estimates that it spends less than $700,000 annually to inspect catfish processing facilities, and NMFS inspection services pose no additional cost to the federal government because its costs are covered by industry service fees. FSIS estimates that the implementation of its proposed catfish inspection program would cost the federal government

---

[19]GAO-11-286.

and industry an additional $14 million annually. As estimated by FSIS, the federal government bears most of the estimated cost, about 98 percent, and industry bears the remaining cost. We did not determine the accuracy of FSIS's estimate, but in our limited review we observed some limitations with FSIS's cost data and assumptions that would affect the final accuracy of the agency's estimate. For example, in its impact analysis, FSIS indicated that it did not have complete information on the total number of domestic and foreign catfish processing facilities that would be affected by the proposed regulations. In addition, the number of countries that will apply for equivalence determination is not known. The number of foreign applicants will, in turn, affect the cost FSIS will incur in making equivalence determinations and in examining shipments at ports of entry. In addition, FSIS may have overstated the federal dollars that FDA and NMFS would save if FSIS implements a catfish inspection program. For example, NMFS officials said that FSIS may have overstated the $1.5 million amount that would be saved if FSIS assumed all inspection duties previously carried out by NMFS inspectors. FDA officials stated that they could not validate the numbers FSIS used to estimate the amount of money FDA would save if FSIS implemented its proposed catfish program. In addition, FSIS estimated that it spent a total of $15.4 million from fiscal years 2009 to 2011 to develop the catfish inspection program, including costs related to catfish sampling studies. In fiscal year 2012, FSIS plans to spend an additional $4.4 million to support further program development.

The cost effectiveness of FSIS's catfish inspection program is unclear. FSIS acknowledges in its risk assessment that there is substantial uncertainty about how effective FSIS's catfish inspection program will be in reducing the prevalence of *Salmonella*-contaminated catfish. In addition, FSIS acknowledged in its risk assessment that it lacks regulatory oversight experience with catfish processing facilities, although it has historically overseen the meat, poultry and processed egg products industries. FDA and NMFS officials we spoke with do not expect FSIS's proposed catfish inspection program to make catfish safer than it already is under current federal oversight programs. Moreover, FSIS would oversee a small fraction of all seafood imports to the United States— about 3 percent—while FDA, using its enhanced authorities, could undertake oversight of all imported seafood.

Conclusion

To implement the catfish inspection requirement in the Farm Bill, FSIS has proposed a program that seeks to mitigate the primary food safety hazard most associated with domestic and imported catfish, which FSIS identified as *Salmonella*. However, the agency's proposed catfish inspection program further fragments the federal oversight system for food safety without demonstrating that there is a problem with catfish or a need for a new federal program. We recognize that FSIS developed this program because it was mandated to do so by the Farm Bill—before FDA received enhanced regulatory authority under FSMA. Even so, FSIS proposed a program that essentially mirrors the catfish oversight efforts already underway by FDA and NMFS. Furthermore, since FDA introduced HACCP requirements for seafood processing facilities—including catfish facilities—in 1997, no reported outbreaks of illnesses caused by *Salmonella* contamination of catfish have been reported—the hazard identified by FSIS—indicating the low risk presented by this pathogen in catfish. Consequently, if implemented, the catfish inspection program would likely not enhance the safety of catfish but would duplicate FDA and NMFS inspections at a cost to taxpayers. With FDA's new authority under FSMA, the federal government has an opportunity to enhance the effectiveness of the food safety system of all imported seafood, including catfish, and avoid the duplication of effort and costs that would result from FSIS's implementation of its proposed catfish inspection program.

Matter for Congressional Consideration

To enhance the effectiveness of the food safety system for catfish and avoid duplication of effort and cost, Congress should consider repealing provisions of the Farm Bill that assigned USDA responsibility for examining and inspecting catfish and for creating a catfish inspection program.

Agency Comments and Our Evaluation

We provided USDA and the Departments of Commerce and Health and Human Services with a draft of this report for their review and comment. We also provided a draft of this report to the Department of State, the Office of the U.S. Trade Representative, and the Office of Management and Budget. On April 25, 2012, we received written comments from USDA, which are reproduced in appendix II. USDA and the Department of Health and Human Services provided technical comments, which we incorporated as appropriate. The Department of Commerce did not provide written comments.

USDA stated that it appreciated our work in planning, conducting, and issuing the report. USDA added that it is committed to completing the rulemaking process on catfish inspection in a manner that is consistent with the 2008 Farm Bill provisions.

As agreed with your offices, unless you publicly announce the contents of this report earlier, we plan no further distribution until 30 days from the report date. At that time, we will send copies to the appropriate congressional committees; the Secretaries of Agriculture, Commerce, Health and Human Services, and State; the U.S. Trade Representative; the Director of the Office of Management and Budget; and other interested parties. In addition, the report will be available at no charge on the GAO website at http://www.gao.gov.

If you or your staff have any questions about this report, please contact me at (202) 512-3841 or shamesl@gao.gov. Contact points for our Offices of Congressional Relations and Public Affairs may be found on the last page of this report. Key contributors to this report are listed in appendix III.

Lisa Shames
Director, Natural Resources and Environment

Appendix I: Scope and Methodology

We were asked to examine the U.S. Department of Agriculture's (USDA) Food Safety Inspection Service's (FSIS) proposed catfish inspection program. Our objectives were to determine (1) how FSIS determined that *Salmonella* presented the primary food safety hazard in catfish and (2) the anticipated impact of FSIS's proposed catfish inspection program on other federal food safety inspection programs.

To address the first objective, we reviewed documents FSIS had prepared including the draft risk assessment that assessed the hazards associated with consuming catfish. We also reviewed information on the Food and Drug Administration's (FDA) import refusals for imported catfish prepared by USDA's Economic Research Service for 1998 through August 2010. We also reviewed the results of FSIS's preliminary microbiological testing of catfish samples conducted in 2011. We interviewed officials from FSIS, FDA, and the National Marine Fisheries Service (NMFS) to better understand the food safety hazard catfish presents and the information FSIS presented in its draft risk assessment. We also interviewed officials from the Office of the U.S. Trade Representative, the Department of State, and the Office of Management and Budget. To gain stakeholders' perspectives on the food safety hazards that catfish present, we reviewed comments provided to FSIS during the public comment period. We also spoke with representatives from the Catfish Farmers of America, National Fisheries Institute, the Association of Food and Drug Officials, and the Center for Science in the Public Interest.

To assess the anticipated impact of FSIS's proposed catfish inspection program on other federal food safety inspection programs, we reviewed the proposed regulations for the catfish inspection program and other agency documents including the preliminary regulatory impact analysis that describe the proposed program and the costs and benefits expected by FSIS after implementation. We reviewed the FDA Food Safety Modernization Act to identify the additional authorities to enhance the oversight of imported seafood this legislation granted FDA. We interviewed officials from FSIS, FDA, and NMFS to better understand FSIS's proposed program, its costs and benefits, and the similarities and differences between it and FDA and NMFS inspection programs. In our review of FDA and NMFS inspection programs, we also gathered information on program costs. To gain stakeholders' perspectives on FSIS's proposed regulations for continuous catfish inspection, we reviewed comments from industry and consumer groups provided to FSIS during the public comment period. We spoke with representatives of the Catfish Farmers of America and the National Fisheries Institute. We also spoke with representatives of two domestic seafood processors that process both catfish and other seafood during site visits to their facilities in Massachusetts to gain their perspectives on the potential impact of the proposed regulations on their operations. We reviewed past GAO reports relevant to this topic.

In addition, we analyzed Department of Commerce data on imported seafood, including catfish, for 2010. We present these data as background to illustrate the relative volume of catfish and other seafood. We also analyzed USDA National Agricultural Statistics Service data on catfish processing to illustrate trends in domestic catfish production and imports from 2006 to 2010, also as background. For both of these data sets we reviewed existing documentation about these data and any limitations. We found both data sets to be sufficiently reliable for the above-mentioned purposes.

We conducted this performance audit from June 2011 to May 2012 in accordance with generally accepted government auditing standards. Those standards require that we plan and perform the audit to obtain sufficient, appropriate evidence to provide a reasonable basis for our findings and conclusions based on our audit objectives. We believe that the evidence obtained provides a reasonable basis for our findings and conclusions based on our audit objectives.

Appendix II: Comments from the U.S. Department of Agriculture

DEPARTMENT OF AGRICULTURE
OFFICE OF THE SECRETARY
WASHINGTON, D.C. 20250

April 24, 2012

Ms. Lisa Shames
Director
Natural Resources and Environment
United States Government Accountability Office
441 G Street, N.W.
Washington, D.C. 20538

Dear Ms. Shames:

The United States Department of Agriculture (USDA) appreciates the opportunity to review the U.S. Government Accountability Office's (GAO) draft report entitled, "Seafood Safety: Responsibility for Catfish Safety Should Be Transferred from USDA to FDA" (12-411). USDA appreciates GAO's work in planning, conducting and issuing this report.

The Department, specifically the Food Safety and Inspection Service (FSIS), is currently proposing regulations requiring continuous inspection of catfish and catfish products. FSIS is proposing these regulations to implement provisions of the Food, Conservation, and Energy Act (Farm Bill) of 2008. Although the GAO draft report does not contain any recommendations specifically directed at USDA, the Department, specifically FSIS, remains committed to completing the rulemaking process on catfish inspection in a manner that is consistent with the Farm Bill provisions.

Again, thank you for the opportunity to review and comment on this draft report. Technical comments were submitted under separate cover. We look forward to working with you on future Department of Agriculture engagements.

Sincerely,

Brian Ronholm
Deputy Under Secretary
Food Safety

Appendix III: GAO Contact and Staff Acknowledgments

GAO Contact	Lisa Shames, (202) 512-3481 or shamesl@gao.gov
Staff Acknowledgments	In addition to the individual named above, Anne K. Johnson (Assistant Director), David Moreno (Analyst-in-Charge), Michele Sahlhoff, Carol Herrnstadt Shulman, Swati Sheladia Thomas, and Kiki Theodoropoulos made key contributions to this report. Important contributions were also made by Kevin Bray, Michele Fejfar, Jose Alfredo Gomez, and Jena Sinkfield.

GAO's Mission	The Government Accountability Office, the audit, evaluation, and investigative arm of Congress, exists to support Congress in meeting its constitutional responsibilities and to help improve the performance and accountability of the federal government for the American people. GAO examines the use of public funds; evaluates federal programs and policies; and provides analyses, recommendations, and other assistance to help Congress make informed oversight, policy, and funding decisions. GAO's commitment to good government is reflected in its core values of accountability, integrity, and reliability.
Obtaining Copies of GAO Reports and Testimony	The fastest and easiest way to obtain copies of GAO documents at no cost is through GAO's website (www.gao.gov). Each weekday afternoon, GAO posts on its website newly released reports, testimony, and correspondence. To have GAO e-mail you a list of newly posted products, go to www.gao.gov and select "E-mail Updates."
Order by Phone	The price of each GAO publication reflects GAO's actual cost of production and distribution and depends on the number of pages in the publication and whether the publication is printed in color or black and white. Pricing and ordering information is posted on GAO's website, http://www.gao.gov/ordering.htm. Place orders by calling (202) 512-6000, toll free (866) 801-7077, or TDD (202) 512-2537. Orders may be paid for using American Express, Discover Card, MasterCard, Visa, check, or money order. Call for additional information.
Connect with GAO	Connect with GAO on Facebook, Flickr, Twitter, and YouTube. Subscribe to our RSS Feeds or E-mail Updates. Listen to our Podcasts. Visit GAO on the web at www.gao.gov.
To Report Fraud, Waste, and Abuse in Federal Programs	Contact: Website: www.gao.gov/fraudnet/fraudnet.htm E-mail: fraudnet@gao.gov Automated answering system: (800) 424-5454 or (202) 512-7470
Congressional Relations	Katherine Siggerud, Managing Director, siggerudk@gao.gov, (202) 512-4400, U.S. Government Accountability Office, 441 G Street NW, Room 7125, Washington, DC 20548
Public Affairs	Chuck Young, Managing Director, youngc1@gao.gov, (202) 512-4800 U.S. Government Accountability Office, 441 G Street NW, Room 7149 Washington, DC 20548

Please Print on Recycled Paper.